Sufi Message

of

Unity of Religious Ideals

Hidayat Inayat-Khan, the third child of Sufi Master Hazrat Inayat Khan and Ora Ray Baker-Bernard, is a well-known music composer and conductor. He followed his family's musical tradition, of which his great-grandfather Maula Bakhsh and his father Inayat Khan were the highlights, and was violinist in different orchestras and string quartets. He is the creator of the Message Symphony, the Gandhi Symphony, and many other works like the Suite Symphonique. Also, he was a Professor of music at the Lycee Musical de Dieulefit, France and, later, in Holland.

At an age when people normally retire from work, Hidayat Inayat-Khan accepted the leadership of the Sufi Movement as its Representative General and Pir-o-Murshid, in complete dedication to its founder, his father, Hazrat Inayat Khan.

Sufi Message

of

Unity of Religious Ideals

Hidayat Inayat-Khan

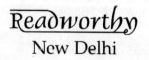

Readworthy
New Delhi

Copyright © Author

All rights reserved. Without limiting the rights under copyright reserved above, no part of this publication may be reproduced, utilized, stored in or introduced into a retrieval system, or transmitted, in any form or by any means (electronic, mechanical, photocopying, recording, or otherwise), without the prior written permission of both the copyright owner and the publisher.

Disclaimer from the author: All religions/beliefs and schools of philosophy are equally respected and statement of any kind does not endorse or prefer one over the other. The beliefs, thoughts, convictions, suitability, benefits, etc. expressed are all personal to me. Any narration, belief, indication, conclusion, method or similar statement should not be construed as recommendations. Those may and would not suit to all or even anybody in some cases. These are not to be taken as a panacea. Nothing is promised. The reader may or may not follow what is stated; he or she may do so only by using his or her own personal discretion and at his or her own responsibility.

The views expressed in this volume are those of the author(s) and are not necessarily those of the publisher.

First published 2012

Readworthy Publications (P) Ltd.

Editorial Office	Sales Office
B-65, Mansa Ram Park	4735/22, Prakash Deep Building,
Near Master Palace	Ground Floor, Ansari Road, Daryaganj
New Delhi–110 059-07	New Delhi–110 002-02
Phone: 011-2533 3244	Phone: 011-43549197

Email: info@readworthypub.com   Web: www.readworthypub.com

Cataloging in Publication Data--DK
Courtesy: D.K. Agencies (P) Ltd. <docinfo@dkagencies.com>

Khan, Hidayat, 1917-
   Sufi message of unity of religious ideals / Hidayat Inayat-
Khan.

   p.   cm.

   ISBN 13: 978-93-5018-134-8   ISBN 10: 93-5018-134-7

   1. Sufism. 2. Religions--Relations.   I. Title.

DDC 297.4   23

Printed at Salasar Imaging Systems, Delhi-35

Foreword

Hidayat Inayat-Khan has gifted us with this book which is a powerful and potent distillation of the spiritual heritage handed down from his father, Hazrat Inayat Khan, founder the Sufi Movement in 1923. This book is written with great clarity and quintessential substance—the Sufi Message. It subtly, and at the same time remarkably, highlights the 'universal' quality of the 'Message' for it articulates the connections between this universal Sufism Message and Hinduism, Yoga, Zoroastrianism, and other spiritual and religious traditions.

This is an important text because it opens the realm of Sufism beyond the confines of classicism towards a greater understanding of the universality of the Sufi Message as given by Hazrat Inayat Khan.

The universal quality of the Sufi Message is highlighted by the following words of Hazrat Inayat Khan.

"Sufism in itself is no religion nor even a culture as a distinct or definite doctrine. There is no better explanation of Sufism than saying that any person who has a knowledge of life outside and within is a Sufi. Therefore, there has not been in any period of the world's history a founder or an exponent of Sufism, but Sufism has been all the time. No doubt, as far as we can trace, we find that since the time of Abraham there have been esoteric schools; many of them were called Sufi schools. The Sufi schools of Arabia had Arabic culture; it was more metaphysical. The Sufi schools of Persia developed more the literary aspect; and the Sufi schools of India developed meditative faculty, but the truth and the ideal have remained the same as the central theme of Sufism in all these schools."

This book represents the concentrated essence of the entire body of work of Hazrat Inayat Khan in a pithy, comprehendible and accessible form.

Professor Nuria Stephanie Anne Sabato

Introduction

Sufi Movement

Hazrat Inayat Khan gave the name 'Sufi Movement' to the organization, which is working for the spreading of the message in our time. The term 'Movement' describes an accommodation to all circumstances and changes in the continual progress in the way of life in the world.

Universal Worship

The 'Universal Worship' is a ceremony in which all religions are symbolically represented: Hindism, Buddhism, Zoroastrianism, Judauism, Christianity, Islam and all those known and unknown to the world. This ceremony is inspired by the great ideals of love, harmony and beauty.

Beloved Ones of God

'Beloved Ones of God' are the words with which Hazrat Inayat Khan always greeted his audience, whether the audience was one of Christians, Jews, Buddhists, Hindus or Muslims. These magic words were like a historical call for 'Unity of religious ideals,' launched for the first time in religious history.

Unity of Religious Ideals

Unity of Religious Ideals does not mean mixing all religions together as one impersonal concept. It means respecting all religions at their own level of expression. It is obvious that following misinterpretations by the followers, the original ideals symbolically formulated in all religions, gradually degenerated in speculative dogmas, conventions, regulations and theories.

Spiritual Liberty

Another historical concept, expressed by Hazrat Inayat Khan is the call for 'Spiritual Liberty'. Those two words, which had never been placed together—representing as historical formulation relating to 'Spirituality'—are so positively contrary to religious indoctrination or to the working in conservative orders, where the power of the leader is dominant.

Hazrat Inayat Khan often said that there are as many truths as there are pilgrims searching for Truth; and when one believes in the pure spirit of one's own religion, one then discovers that same spirit as the source of inspiration seen originally in all religions.

Contents

1

The Message in Our Time

The message in our time is not meant for only a certain culture nor is it for just one part of the world; it is destined for the whole of humanity. This message of the unity of religious ideals could be symbolically illustrated as a Universal Worship, inspired by the history of the great religions, known and unknown to the world at large.

To the question, 'What is the Message?' the answer varies in accordance with the understanding, because each person represents a different point of view, yet all claim to drink from the same water of truth, whether it be called a stream, a river, a lake, a sea, an ocean or the Divine Source itself.

The word message could be understood as abstract energy that becomes intelligible to humanity through the inspiration of all those, down the ages, who have brought one and the same message, and whose magnetism still resonates in the hearts of the devotees, varying in accordance to the interpretation given to the original word. The preservation of that resonance has always depended upon a continuous renewal of the original inspiration; and the characteristics of those renewals have always been related to the living conditions, rules and cultures in the areas where they expanded. The mission of those renewals could be identified by the term 'Religion.'

The world messengers have come with the great ideal of liberating humanity from the diversifications of speculative theories related to mystifications of abstract concepts, that have persisted through centuries, maintaining the specter of fanaticism even in this age when science has successfully catapulted factual knowledge as far as the surface of the moon.

Religious structures, which arise from spiritual ideals, have always been intended to offer a helping hand toward the realization of Truth, but regrettably, these high ideals tend to be limited within endless cultural forms and to be clad in artificial garments by those who do not see that the means to attain an object cannot be the goal; the goal is further still. The path is the means of reaching the goal, but if one argues over the authenticity of the path, one is misled by the differences and can never really reach anywhere.

Each religion strikes a characteristic tone, and when all blend harmoniously together as a divine symphony, one then encounters the reality of a perfect unity of all spiritual ideals. However, this does not mean indulging in a federative initiative; it only means discovering the golden thread running through all religious structures, which reveals a profound spiritual oneness in the original inspiration, interwoven within all religious ideals.

A religion, which is the materialization of the original message, is continually reshaped over time, according to the understanding of various cultural reformers, in words and forms adapted to the educational standards of the multitude, whereas the parallel development of science has always been focused on the search for definable facts, structured according to logical definitions.

Through the centuries, the moral and spiritual claims of religious theories have been diversely interpreted by the 'callers from the pulpit', and still today are understood in various ways by the followers of the followers who do not realize that these interpretations have little in common with the spiritual origin of the sacred word.

Spirituality, which is the essence of all religions, cannot be framed within doctrines nor defined in words, nor can it be taught or learned; it can only be discovered by way of the heart. Therefore, spirituality really means rebirth, in the sense that one begins to discover that it has always been one's birthright, and it could best be described as the perfume of true knowledge.

The Sufi Message in our time, which is inspired by spiritual ideals, is neither a new religion nor a cult, neither is it a doctrine nor a secret institution. Perhaps one could say that it is the same religion of the heart that has always been, ever since wisdom was wisdom. Therefore, the term 'Sufi', meaning wisdom, refers not only to ancient orders, known or unknown, that have blossomed through the ages, but also indicates the purification of the mind from pre-conceived ideas and illogical thinking, especially with regard to abstract concepts.

The Sufi Message is the answer to the cry of humanity calling for Spiritual Liberty beyond all distinctions and differences; it is a message of brotherhood and sisterhood inspired by the all-pervading enfoldment of love, harmony and beauty.

May the sacred Ka'aba Stone, which Abraham, Father of three great religious streams, placed thousands of years ago as a Temple of Initiation to symbolize the ideal of One and the same God, be forever an example of dignity and respect for all those venturing on the path of Truth, making no distinction of religion or belief.

2

Unity of Religious Ideals

The followers of all religions believe in wisdom. Christians feel that there is wisdom in being Christian; Jews feel that there is wisdom in being Jewish; Muslims feel that there is wisdom in being Muslim; Hindus and Buddhists as well as the followers of so many other religions known or unknown to the world also feel that there is wisdom in the religion to which they are attracted. Nevertheless, each one who truly discovers wisdom is relieved thereby from identifying with the limitations of religious differences.

Wisdom, which raises above all distinctions and differences, is in itself the truest definition of the term religious insight. Wisdom is not a religion, nor is it a cult or a school; wisdom is an 'open door', an attitude of inner sympathy towards all beliefs, recognizing the illusions in all speculative interpretation of Truth.

Truth, however, is not necessarily what one might think it to be. It is not glimpsed only in physical experience, nor solely seen in thought, nor found in the feeling heart alone, but is only revealed fully at a still higher level of consciousness, where boundaries vanish and the self no longer separates reality from illusion. It is a level where there are neither limitations nor opposites, with no relationship to any framework of preconceived ideas, such as those expressed in all dogmatic interpretations of Truth. There are as many Truths as there are seekers after Truth.

If one took six or seven different glasses, each of a different colour, and poured water in them, the water would appear red in red glass, blue in blue glass, green in a green glass, and so on, although it would be the same water in each.

In the same way, all religions are in their origin of divine inspiration, but, like the image of water in different coloured glasses, as soon as heavenly inspiration is reflected in human thought, it acquires the colour of that thinking. We then call one colour Hinduism, another Buddhism, another Islam and still other colours are called Judaism, Christianity, and other religious denominations.

Therefore, since the origin of all religions is of divine nature, they can only be understood inasmuch as one is prepared to recognize in each one the unity of religious ideals. At this level of understanding, all religions appear to be so many derivations of one and the same impulse, the cry of the heart, the longing of the soul for Truth. All religions, which manifest periodically as sparks of light, have been inspired in all times by the all-pervading message of compassion that has always been and shall always be offered to mankind.

The religious reformers formulated their teachings on the level of the cultural standards of the followers, but from age to age, the moral and spiritual values of religions are variously interpreted by the 'callers from the pulpit', and also variously understood by the followers of the followers, who go on forever pursuing one dogma after another, not realizing that these do not always have anything in common with the original word. When trying to explain God, one fashions an individual concept, limited to the horizon of one's own thinking.

Religious ideals, which were originally offered as a helping hand toward the realization of truth, tend to be confined within different religious forms and to be clad in various illusionary garments by those who do not see that the means to attain an object cannot be the goal; the goal is further still. The path is the means of reaching the goal but if one argues over the authenticity of the path, one is misled by the differences and can never reach the goal.

Each religion strikes a characteristic tone, and when all blend harmoniously together as a divine symphony, one then encounters the reality of a perfect unity of all spiritual ideals. However, this does not mean indulging in a federative initiative; it only means discovering the golden thread running through all religious structures, which reveals a profound oneness at the level of the original inspiration, interwoven within all religious expressions.

One can only be really attuned to a particular religion if one's heart is open to all religious beliefs, with the same love and understanding for each, and with the understanding that wisdom takes it for granted that some very specific dogmas might have made sense at the time that they were preached, but don't necessarily apply any more in our world today, where science has taken over the responsibility of such subjects as health and education, which used to be part of the basic structures of ancient religion.

Hazrat Inayat Khan came to us with a call for the unity of religious ideals. This call implies being liberated from such feelings as 'my religion' as opposed to 'your religion,' because there is only one religion and several interpretations of the one Truth. Through the ages there is one religion after another, but each one came as a confirmation of the previous one.

The religion of our time is destined to be the religion of the heart, and since there are many hearts, there are many religions, although all religions spring forth from one and the same heart, the temple of God, wherein, when wisdom prevails, Love, Lover and Beloved are one.

3

Sufism

Sufism is neither a religion nor a cult nor a sect, nor is it only from the East nor from the West. Sufism means wisdom, and one could say that Sufism is the same message of the heart that has always been, ever since wisdom was wisdom. It is an open door to Truth, with sympathy towards all beliefs, while at the same time avoiding speculation upon abstract concepts.

A Sufi believes in the Divine origin of every form of worship in which the unity of religious ideals is respected. Therefore, the term 'Sufi' does not refer only to ancient schools, known or unknown, where spiritual ideas have blossomed within various orders through the ages, but the term Sufi also indicates wisdom as understood by the purification of the mind and the opening of the doors of the heart.

When pronouncing the word 'Sufism,' the '-ism' tends to suggest a limited understanding of wisdom, but wisdom can never be defined. For a Sufi, there are just as many expressions of wisdom as there are seekers after wisdom. Sufism is an attitude, a path. It is the path of love for mankind. It is not a speculative adventure; there is no searching after phenomena.

Sufism does not mean being any better than anybody else. Sufism means to be a human being, so that others might perhaps benefit from the experience. When offering as a brother or a sister to partake in easing the burden of misunderstandings between believers, the Sufi uses the language of spiritual liberty to communicate sympathy and dedication in support of various understandings of the one ideal of worship.

The light of the glowing sun cannot be limited to just one ray. That light shines in an infinite number of rays. In the same way, the light of Truth is not only reserved for the so-called spiritual ones; it shines in the hearts of everyone. Nevertheless, the brilliancy of that light varies in its intensity, dependent upon the transparency of the ego.

The Sufi teachings are focused upon the Spirit of Guidance, the Teacher of all teachers; the source of inspiration to the world of science, of creativity to the world of art, and human rights to the social world. To the religious world, this message calls aloud for the unity of spiritual ideals, which is the necessary condition for raising human understanding to a level of spiritual awakening.

The Sufi emblem is a flying heart, symbolically representing the great power of love as it reaches upwards, carried upon wings of 'Spiritual Liberty' into the spheres of Divine Consciousness. In this symbol, the five-pointed star represents the light of the spirit of guidance, illuminating the way all along the journey toward inner awakening. The crescent moon represents the receptive and expressive qualities of the heart set free when the limited self is no more the spectator.

The religion in our time is destined to be a Universal Message of Unity. Upon the altar of the 'Unity of Religious Ideals', the burning lights represent the great world religions, as well as all those who, whether known or unknown to the world, have held aloft the light of Truth through the darkness of human ignorance. A further aspect of the Universal Worship is the offering of passages from various holy scriptures placed side by side, with the object of discovering the similarity found in all, provided that the teachings are received at a spiritual level of understanding.

During this sacred ceremony, the blessings of all the great masters are profoundly felt when one's heart is open to the pure essence of all religious inspirations, and when these are seen as so many rays of light coming from one and the same source, which is destined to shine for the welfare of all humanity.

What is really experienced in worship?

What is really understood by prayer, contemplation and meditation?

Is it not, perhaps, the call of the heart?

The spiritual path is a process of tuning the heart to an inner pitch, which is only heard when the doors of the heart are open, and the absence of the self miraculously reveals the silent tone within. This process can be traced in all religious teachings, and in this process lies the whole secret of happiness and inner peace.

What is the heart?

Is it not the temple of God?

And if so, could we really venture to invite the Divine Presence into that temple if impurities such as the 'I am' concept are there, along with all our doubts and fears and wants?

But what does this all really mean?

It means that as beloved ones of God we are expected to remind ourselves of the noble responsibilities, which are ours. It is then that one might eventually discover that God-consciousness, which one had been frantically pursuing, is in fact already there. But so long as this consciousness is not in attunement with the heart, then whatever is the external appearance of spirituality, piety or morality, this all remains void of Godliness.

If God-consciousness could be explained at all, it is certainly an unconditional reality of love, human and Divine; and it is with the great power of this profound realization that all brothers and sisters of all convictions humbly unite in love, harmony and beauty.

4

The Alchemy of Happiness

Perhaps there is a secret key to resolve the paradox in which the self-created ego is constantly defocusing itself from the true self within. This psychological misconception of reality generates complexes where one makes oneself unhappy within the horizon of one's own restricted mind-world, as well as being a nuisance to others. When continually focusing on the negative things in others, one only destroys one's own happiness.

There is no happiness when forcing others to agree with one's own opinion, but one can force oneself to try to understand where differences separate. Happiness cannot be found under the pressure of possessiveness. It is only there when one is ready to offer it without expecting or demanding anything in return. When realizing how privileged one is to be the Beloved one of God, one's consciousness is raised to a higher level than just want to be happy.

This process is traditionally known as the 'Alchemy of Happiness'. In this connection, one can imagine oneself facing a closed door, knowing that on the other side precious vases containing happiness can be reached, but the key to the door must be found.

That mysterious door symbolizes the door to the heart, and the key symbolizes the sword of wisdom with which the ego is to be vanquished.

There are golden keys, silver keys, copper keys and iron keys, but one also needs to know how to use the key once one has found it. All esoteric methods have their qualities but what is important is to be aware of what type of self-discipline practised, and what is the true purpose of the efforts made?

If no accomplishment is discovered on the path of the 'Alchemy of Happiness', one might be tempted to simply break open that symbolical door, but to one's disappointment, the precious vases would also be destroyed, and nothing would remain other than one's own restless and untamable ego.

When wanting to be happy there are quite a number of conditions to be met with, such as: appreciation for all that one has and having compassion for those who have less; overcoming unreasonable jealousy which is comparable to a lock on the doors of the heart; being aware that happiness cannot be obtained at the cost of the suffering of others; resisting self assertion and false pretence which only lead to failure. Mastery over this dilemma can be accomplished through endless struggles with the ego, steadily confronting this iron façade with the flames of love offered to others without any expectation of return.

When envying others, it should well be remembered that, although one might have less happiness than those whom one envies, one would sooner or later have to pay an even higher price than one would have expected for that same happiness. And what is more, true happiness cannot be obtained at the cost of the suffering of others. When wanting happiness for one's self, one is faced by quite a number of necessary conditions, such as sincerely appreciating all that one has been granted, and having compassion for those who are not so privileged as oneself. There is a difference between being happy as the result of a particular circumstance, or being in an unconditional state of happiness, where one's consciousness is raised to a higher level than just the 'I' concept.

Happiness is a privilege. It is also our birthright. Therefore, it certainly is our duty to be happy, but this is only possible when offering happiness to others without expecting anything in return. This golden key to happiness implies absolute absence of self-assertion and self-pretence. Among the many reasons for not being happy, the principal one is lack of sense of appreciation. Displeasure as a result of one's own pessimistic attitude causes obstructions which could be overcome with wisdom, will-power, perseverance and insight into one's own misjudgments, rather than blaming others for one's unhappiness.

When wanting happiness just for one's self, one is constantly confronted by those who are not so privileged by circumstances, as well as also by those who have been favoured by Destiny's grace, which is unconditionally bestowed upon the chosen ones, and which does have its price to pay at the level of responsibilities, encountered unexpectedly on the path.

Fortunately, the seekers of happiness dispose of free will, and with that power, we all possess consciously or unconsciously the secret of happiness, for which we are destined.

5

Wisdom

Wisdom might perhaps be described as being an attitude of compassion but cannot be defined in words, for there are just as many expressions of wisdom as there are seekers of wisdom. Yet, for the one who is really wise there is only one wisdom, although there are many different ways of understanding that one wisdom, and different forms of expression through which the one and only wisdom is recognized by the wise.

As soon as one attempts to define abstract concepts, one gets taken away into the labyrinth of one's own thoughts, which break down into speculative descriptions, and one builds up one's own dogmatic ideas which are then added to the many which one picks up through one's experiences, together with the numerous impressions and influences which constitute the mind world. Then when one starts putting one's beliefs and understandings into words, the words tend to deviate from the original ideas which were themselves only arbitrary concepts, and the result of all this is so often presented as being the one and only truth.

Perhaps one might discover someday what it really means to be wise, when realizing that things are just as important as is one's attachment to them. Nothing is really important, and yet, everything is important. But that which seems so important to oneself does not always seem important to others.

The wise remain free from judging others and from specifying what is good and what is bad. Good and bad are concepts that can only be determined according to one's own conscience. Therefore, at a higher level of understanding, the only guidance to what is right or wrong for oneself is ones own conscience. When one does something inappropriate one is unhappy and even though one might try to fool oneself, one always really knows what is right and what is wrong.

One usually thinks that one's thoughts are only inside the head, and that emotions are only within the chest, but in fact thoughts extend throughout the indefinable sphere of consciousness, and the emotions expand indefinitely, unlimited by concepts such as time, space and intellectual logic.

6

Brotherhood and Sisterhood

We all know that brothers and sisters certainly experience quarrelling in the early years. It is healthy, because it is the most natural way of learning how to get along with others at a later stage in life. In what way does this relate to the ideal of brotherhood and sisterhood?

One could perhaps say that the great ideal of brotherhood and sisterhood can only be experienced while being aware of one's own shortcomings, rather than while making a display of those of others. There are so many wonderful souls who try to help others, but how can one possibly help solve the problems of others if one cannot solve one's own problems?

It is only when the ego is held in check, that one might discover a spark of beauty in one's brother or sister, so that it reflects back upon oneself, gradually awakening in the feeling heart sympathetic feelings, which purify one of all prejudices.

Basic principles such as love, harmony and beauty only appear in action when one refrains from imposing one's own ideas upon others. Reversely, others might eventually be impressed by a worthwhile opinion. As it has been said: "The wise have two opinions, their own, and that of the other." How can one expect others to have understanding for one's own opinion if one does not have understanding for theirs?

Even if one does not agree with the opinion of another, one might remember that they have the right not to agree with one's own opinion. It is wise to respect the fact that others have different opinions than one's own, without adopting them. But when respecting them one enriches one's own opinions.

Mastery means having discipline over one's self, as opposed to imposing one's will upon others. This means attuning oneself to a higher level of understanding, which is so beautifully revealed in the words of Jesus Christ, Who said: "Search ye not the speck in the eye of the other, but rather the log in your own eye." There is a natural gift of free will granted in the ability to leave it to one's own heart to sense the truth behind all illusions.

What does it matter in what country one was born, or in what culture or religion one was raised? What is important is the understanding for each other, beyond all circumstances and differences. Each one lives in the way which has been adopted, and consequently, there are many lessons to learn from each other's, which either lead to inner peace or to unfavourable consequences for oneself and for those with whom one is destined to live.

There is so much incomprehension in the world and there is so much craving to compete at all levels of our society. In response to this all, let us rise above our own limited visions of Truth, which cannot be proven; it is untruth that tries to prove itself.

Let us attune ourselves to the great stream of love that spreads beyond all borders; and in our longing for harmony among brothers and sisters on the path, we shall discover that we are all as so many drops of one and the same ocean of Truth.

7

Esoteric Practices

Hazrat Inayat Khan offered us his teaching 90 years ago, in a time when very few people in the Western World had any knowledge of Hindu yoga or Sufi mysticism, whereas today many publications openly disclose ancient esoteric methods known for ages by yogis and mystics; and obviously, we might be questioned at any time as to the similarities between Sufi practices and those of other traditions. Therefore, as representatives of the Message in our time, it is good to be aware of certain parallels between Hindu yoga and Sufi mysticism. For example, Zikar is the parallel of Japa; Purification breaths and Kassab are the parallel of Pranayama; Wazifa is the parallel of Mantra; Shaghal is the parallel of Mudra yoga; Nidra yoga is the parallel of Amal, and several other Sufi practices are also parallel of various historical yoga traditions.

Paradoxically, it is in the understanding of these parallels that we discover the importance of pursuing the initial practices given to us by our initiators, which carry along with them the blessings received at the moment of initiation. Nevertheless, certain additional practices can offer a growing enrichment as we travel onwards, just as the first letters of the alphabet that we learned in our early years were followed at a later stage by the knowledge of words, and subsequently the technique of forming sentences and paragraphs.

Obviously, neither paragraphs nor sentences nor words could ever be co-ordinated in our minds without having attuned ourselves initially to the letters of the alphabet that constitute the basis of communication in our daily lives. Similarly, the first practices given are so important in the process of the inner awakening, which is perceived and expressed when experiencing those fundamental esoteric practices.

We might discover someday, by the help of esoteric practices, that there is no such thing as darkness. The difference between light and darkness is only a difference of intensity of light. A dim lamp radiates less brightly than a powerful one does, although both are connected to the same wiring system, with the same voltage. The difference is that each lamp responds according to its own capacity. Each one of us could be seen as an individual lamp receiving the same current of Divine guidance, yet the brightness of the light varies in accordance with the inner condition of our hearts and the degree of transparency of the chakras. Divine guidance is always present, silently helping us inasmuch as we are awakened to the reality of that guidance.

8

The Gentle Singing Zikar
of Hazrat Inayat Khan

We all know the beautiful, ancient Sufi words, "My heart is an empty bowl in which there is only place for Thee." This picture helps understand the mystical process followed in the Singing Zikar.

There are numberless ancient melodies employed in India, in the Middle East and in many other countries to accompany the words '*La el la ha el Allah hu.*' Each of these melodies corresponds to the vibrations of time and place and has inspired thousands and thousands of followers over the ages.

Hazrat Inayat Khan created his own melody for the words of the Singing Zikar, which awakens serene vibrations, as well as a very uplifting effect within the feeling heart. It is certainly to be understood that out of great devotion we feel so privileged to adopt this special melody, as an accompaniment to what is now known as the 'Gentle Singing Zikar', and to which every sincere seeker is welcome.

The gentle Singing Zikar is sustained by a musical recording, the reason being that it is important to keep the musical pitch constant, for it would otherwise naturally descend; and also to maintain a steady tempo throughout. However, we must not confuse the Singing Zikar pratice with other types of Wazifa Zikars, which are recited in various ways.

Furthermore, in different countries there are specific ways of pronouncing words according to various cultures, and consequently the words of the Zikar, *La el la ha el Allah hu*, are sometimes pronounced differently. Some pronounce those words as *il Allah hu*, and other pronounce the same words as *al Allah hu* or *ayl Allah hu*. Hazrat Inayat Khan followed the ancient Persian pronunciation, from the time of Rumi, which is *el Allah hu*, and which he explained as "Specific vibration of the Message in our time."

The music notes written in Hazrat Inayat Khan's own handwriting are sacredly preserved in the Sufi Movement Museum, together with the ancient mechanical metronome with which the beats of the Singing Zikar were kept at a given tempo when it was done collectively.

Another particularity of the gentle Singing Zikar, as taught to mureeds in the early days, is that it is done either sitting cross-legged on the floor, or sitting on a chair, depending upon one's physical condition. If sitting upon a chair, one sits on the edge of the seat, so that the body is not leaning on the back of the chair, and in either case, the palms of the hands are placed upon the knees, thereby closing a magnetic circuit.

The rotating movement is done with the whole torso and not by only twisting the neck, which explains why the body must not lean against anything. Another point to consider is that the movement is a circular one, starting on the left side with the chin inclined toward the heart. With closed eyes one then traces a circular movement, going from left to right, rising upward and returning again downward toward the heart.

In Zikar 1, the chin is lowered back toward the heart upon the words *el Allah hu*, and one stays there feeling the vibrations of the 'hu' sound and visualizing the Divine Presence within the heart until the next repetition begins.

In Zikar 2, the chin is placed upon the heart at the moment of the sound 'hu.'

In Zikar 3, the inclination of the chin toward the heart again corresponds to the sound 'hu.'

In Zikar 4, the circular movement is done with a subtle in-breath through the nose, while on the out-breath one pronounces the sound 'hu,' feeling the vibrations of that sound within the heart.

What is very special in this gentle Singing Zikar is that, as it unfolds through four stages, each stage brings a deeper understanding of what the words *La el la ha-el Allah hu* really convey inwardly. The main purpose of proceeding through these four stages is to gradually wipe out the consciousness of the self, leading to selfless dissolution in the consciousness of the Divine Presence.

The first stage could be understood as a love song to the Divine Presence, expressing the attitude, "O God, I love you."

The second stage corresponds to the feeling of longing, awakened through love, which crystallizes in the call, "Come into my heart."

The third stage awakens a very deep feeling of gratitude and humility, feeling that the Divine Presence has responded to the call and is awakening within.

The fourth stage is a profound meditation where one has forgotten that one was singing a love song to God, and that one called the Divine Presence within. At this stage, one is only conscious of The Divine Presence."

The gentle Singing Zikar meditation ends with a short silence, during which one tries to keep every possible thought out of the mind, only keeping in sight such abstract concepts as bright light and the sound 'hu,' both automatically manifesting above one's head.

During the Singing Zikar, there is no demand, there is no request, there is no want; and at the end of the meditation, one harkens to the all-pervading cosmic tone, and one contemplates upon the all-pervading light, while closing the ears and eyes as done in Mudra yoga. The session then finishes in silence.

9

Initiation and Guidance

"O Seeker, did you know that the 'inner awakening' is like being on a ship, sailing on the great waters of Love, Harmony and Beauty, guided by the compass of the Spirit of Guidance, and driven by the energy of Spiritual Liberty, while heading toward the goal of the annihilation of the ego, where one may begin to realize that the sailor is in reality a ray of the Divine Presence, sailing in the past, present and future on the waves of illusion."

'Initiation' could be understood in many ways, according to the disposition that one has when confronted by the initiative taken as an inner longing. The first step taken at birth is an unconscious initiative, but as the child grows, and all through life, most initiatives are taken consciously.

In other words, life on earth could be seen as a constant succession of initiatives taken. These initiatives, whether material, cultural, or religious, are mostly taken out of free will. If one resists taking an initiative, it may be because it has been imposed upon one, or because the opportunity is misunderstood. Reasoning can also hold one back from taking an initiative which might have successfully fulfilled the purpose. Some initiatives could be understood as reasonable ones, and others as being taken without any logical explanation. Some experiences, which in the past seemed important, become less significant at other stages in life, and show themselves with different values.

As to Initiation, the steps on that path are taken when successfully passing the tests in life, some of which are experienced unconsciously, and others consciously. One faces tests of all natures, wherein one is expected to display such qualities as faith, sincerity, truthfulness, patience, endurance and humility, even if such qualities appear at times unreasonable, odd, meaningless, unkind, or even perhaps unjust. These initiations awaken the urge to meditate upon all that one has discovered in one's relationships with others, assimilating the results with insight, gratitude and understanding.

The subject of initiation has been lavishly discussed, particularly in regard to various esoteric orders, all of which have different methods that consequently give rise to many regrettable misunderstandings. But leaving aside the confusion brought about by so much abuse of the word initiation, this term really suggests taking a step forward, a step taken with hope and courage, with conviction—and this of course implies absolute honesty and truthfulness on the part of both the initiator and the initiate. Obviously, it is difficult for the average person to take the path of initiation, because human nature is such that one wishes to know the likely outcome of any initiative, before one can believe that there is any reality in it.

There are various stages of initiation; the first ones are experienced with the help of guidance, either from that of teachings or by the helpful hand of someone in whom one has put all one's trust. This first step taken could perhaps be understood as one of friendship. However, one must be aware of the risk that one might come in contact with false gurus. Fortunately, with insight and confidence in Divine guidance and when the time has come, one might find some day the honest hand of an initiator whose true friendship shall be appreciated as a blessing from above.

The work of the initiator is to tune those who are open to that which is offered. The initiator is not the player of the instrument but rather the tuner, and when it has been tuned, the instrument is then given into the hands of the player, whose playing becomes more and more clearly the expression of Divine music. On that path there are no rules to follow, because every adept is like a different instrument in the Divine symphony, but there is one basic principle that applies to the manner of life of all concerned, and that is sincerity in humility. The progress depends largely upon the initiate, and one could say that the degree of advancement on the spiritual path is indicated by the expansion of the horizon of consciousness. Unfortunately, in this connection many claim, yet few have truly realized their claim; those who realize do not claim.

A fruitful tree bends the more that its fruits are abundant, and in the same way the deeper the spiritual realization of the initiate, the humbler one becomes. The sincere initiate hardly ever mentions the word initiation, and feels no need to convert others, nor does the initiate have any need for recognition; and if asked what profit is derived by spiritual attunement, the only answer is, in order to become better fitted to serve mankind. To the question whether it is desirable for all to take initiation, the answer would obviously be that every progress in life is worth venturing. Whatever be one's interest in life or one's grade of evolution, it is always advisable to go forward, be it in material, social, religious or spiritual occupations.

The only approach toward inner consciousness is to become sincerely human, or in other words, to be in balance with both the spiritual and material worlds. It is not necessary to seek spirituality in isolation from relationships and duties. It is much more preferable to contemplate and meditate along with one's worldly duties, helping by one's example those who are not conscious of the privileges which are offered to them. The initiate on the spiritual path is not expected to awaken those who are still asleep, but to be prepared to offer a helping hand as soon as the slumbering ones begin to wake. This is basically what is understood by the duty of the initiate.

To the question, what can be expected through initiation, could it be goodness, health, magnetism, insight, or psychological attunement—the answer is that one should never intentionally strive for any of these qualities. The aim is to find peace within, and it is toward this end that through the power of initiation one receives all inspiration and blessings.

Real advancement on the spiritual path goes along with patience and eagerness to progress, notwithstanding the various tests in life and the misunderstandings of one's nearest friends. Furthermore, specific conditions are naturally expected, such as a receptive attitude, and the ability to assimilate apparent and silent teachings received from one's experiences in life without allowing these to be limited by superficial reasoning.

As we know, the word initiation is interpreted in different ways. By some it is understood to be a promotion to a higher grade, and this and many other such explanations make up a catalogue of misunderstandings as to what the word initiation really means. Besides this, there are many different inducements that lead one to initiation; for instance, initiation may come from within when one is inspired by the example of a fellow adept on the path, or when one begins to feel that there is something behind the veil, and that one wishes to make every possible effort to discover that mystery. In such cases one then takes the initiative, or in other words, 'initiation'.

Many often make a great mystery about the word initiation, but it is really very simple: it is the clearing away of past regrets; it is bathing in the sacred waters of inner knowledge; it is making good use of the experiences and powers gained through discipline over one's own ego. There are various paths and methods of attainment, all leading to the same goal, but no initiate will ever reach that goal unless treading upon the path with the two shoes of gratitude and humility. The first and last lesson to learn is that of discipleship. Some might never learn, whereas others learn quickly when attuned to the appropriate attitude.

The initiator does not disturb the inner sleep of the initiate by imposing any obligations, and does not make any claim related to spiritual realization, but only offers a helping hand. The initiator does not use speculative stories regarding spirituality. The language used is clear and meaningful. The spiritual bond between initiator and initiate is a unique example of perfect friendship because it is inspired by an ideal in search of perfection. In this connection the only suitable offering expected from the initiate is whole-hearted confidence and trust; whereas the initiator's offering is appreciative encouragement, bringing into daylight the good sides of the initiate's nature. In so doing, the guidance awakens growing openness in the heart, just as vitalized water enlivens a blossoming plant. It is a harmonious relationship, which secures a balanced understanding at all levels. If the tone of the initiate descends in pitch, the initiator un-assumingly reaches down to the level of the disciple, and in doing so, displays a true example of spiritual democracy. However, constant efforts are expected on both sides to preserve an uplifting relationship in every aspect of study, friendship, mysticism and spiritual awakening.

Initiation is an initiative taken in a direction that is not always understood by others; therefore, there is a need for courage as well as an inner longing, which may not seem to be the way for everyone. The first concern is to guard against one's faith being shaken by opposing and discouraging influences. On this mystical path, steadiness, courage, patience and trust are essential, together with a keen understanding of discipline. How many in the world lack trust, not only in others but also even in themselves? If one cannot trust oneself, how then could one trust others? Trust is a great power. Even if there might be an apparent loss as the result of one's trust, still the power gained thereby is great.

The path of initiation means not only study, but also the recognition of the nobleness of the goal pursued. It is toward this end that one strives with the help of the power of initiation, and it is from within that all inspiration is received. There should be no wall of separation, and if there is one, it must first be removed before one may hope to proceed further, with the heart empty of all else and attuned to the goal one is pursuing. This explains why initiation is at the same time the cry of the heart and the breath that brings to life the object of devotion, insofar as the heart is open to the message that initiation brings.

The effect of a feeling heart can be clearly seen in the lives of great souls, whose deeds and creative accomplishments have been profoundly inspired through their admiration for a great ideal. Those who have really accomplished noble deeds have proceeded with humbleness, greeting at each step forward those who have reached beyond their own goals. Spiritual progress comes with a change of one's point of view, and each step taken upward on the ladder is a new initiation. At each rise, though, one risks being pulled downward again, after which the whole journey must be redone, and at each step upward the fall is greater.

Accomplishment on the path of initiation is obtained through three stages of inner development: unconditional receptivity, deepening of the understanding, and consideration of the law of cause and effect in regard to one's destiny and one's duty to others. In the consideration of others is one's real self expressed, for love's expression is consideration, and love without consideration has no fragrance. Consideration is an attitude that is cultivated in attunement to the music of the heart. If we were to ask ourselves why we are born in human garb rather than remaining as angels in the angelic spheres, perhaps the answer might be that we are here in order to live life fully, in consideration for others and for all things.

There are three main types of 'Life Initiations' unconsciously received: The first one is a natural unfoldment of the soul, an expansion of consciousness that happens without any reason as far as human understanding can perceive. This is called the Grace of God. Another type of initiation comes as the result of great suffering. Like a flash, in a single instant it changes one's whole vision of life. The world has not changed, but like a string stretched by the tuning peg, the initiate has been raised to a higher pitch. The third type of initiation unconsciously received is when losing in a moment's time one's own point of view, one's preconceived ideas, and when seeing from another's point of view, one enlarges one's own, insight, which becomes thereby two-fold: that of the other as well as one's own point of view.

As of the moment of those initiations, all past remorse and sorrow are effaced from thought. There is no reason to grieve further; a new step has been taken and all cruel memories have been left behind. Renunciation is not asked for, but hope and courage are welcomed as one sets forth on the journey toward the goal together with the great family of seekers in the caravan of inner realization. There is also a special blessing in becoming part of the school of inner culture, of which traces are found in every venerable spiritual tradition, and partaking at the same time in the call of the Message in our time, a channel through which flows inspiration offered to the whole of humanity.

There are many who long to guide others on the spiritual path, even though they are not in a position to guide themselves, ignoring that guiding others requires absolute selflessness in every way, and with long years of experience. There is such a thing as having had to deal with problems oneself, so that out of personal experience one is in a position to advise. If one says to a child: do not touch the flame because you shall burn your fingers, the child shall touch it anyway, following a natural tendency to test received advice. It is only after having experienced the pain of a burned finger that the child shall learn the lesson. In the same way, esoteric guidance is of no avail if, out of a lack of trust, the disciple is not prepared to receive guidance.

10

The Art of Personality

When dealing with others, all actions of kindness and consideration are offered without any expectation of return, but the wise take care not to pride themselves upon their good deeds, recognizing that vanity is a veil which dims the light of seeming compassion. It is in the absence of the self, once the kindling spark has grown to a bright flame casting light upon the dark labyrinth of the false ego, that every action becomes a virtue.

Self-denial does not mean turning away from life's duties nor renouncing nature's sources of happiness. Self-denial means to deny that little self which creeps in at every possible occasion. In self-denial, happiness is more intensely appreciated because one has risen above the notion of wanting while taking into consideration one's duties toward the accomplishment of the purpose of one's life.

Happiness means making the right use of those means that have been granted for the purpose of accomplishing the duties expected of us. Unfortunately, our vision of right and wrong is not always correct, nor does it always correspond to the vision of others. Happiness means understanding the wants and needs of our physical body, discovering the many mysteries of the mind, and seeking unfoldment of the loving heart. How few realize that the heart is like a dome within which all, whether good or bad, re-echoes, creating thereby either uplifting or disturbing influences that become in time the characteristics of one's own personality.

Mastery over all impulses is portrayed by the Hindus as a dance at the Court of Indra; every movement of the dance is offered to the Divine Presence. That which the Sufis call the art of personality consists of polishing the rough edges of one's vanity, since vanity is in fact the hidden source from which both virtue and sin arise in one way or other. It is in the practice of this art that the character is ennobled.

The art of personality is like the art of music, wherein ear and voice training are indispensable to determine the pitch of a tone and its interval from another for the purpose of establishing harmony. When applying this same ideal of harmony to one's relations with others, it becomes clear that the beauty of personality shines out in such tendencies as a friendly attitude spontaneously offered in word and action, and in the awakening of a true sense of justice, all of which are expressions of the music of personality.

The art of personality is manifested in all feeling for beauty and sincerity in thought, speech and action. It is revealed in a considerate attitude toward others and in being aware of the re-echo of all that one does in life, for which, sooner or later, one shall have to give an account.

One cannot excuse a negative behavior by saying, "I was only born as a thorn, so how could I be a rose?" Because unlike a plant we are all granted the gift of free will. The beauty, fragrance and colour latent in the root are expressed in the bloom of the rose rather than in the sharp point of the thorn, although rose and thorn are both part of the same plant and have the same root. In the same way, the good qualities latent in human being can be revealed in the beauty and charm of personality.

The charm of the personality, which may give rise to beauty, is also deeply felt in the tone of sincerity, and the secret of this art resides in a perfect balance between both, since a polished manner without sincerity is not really beautiful and frankness without beauty does not reveal the truth in all sincerity.

All disputes and disagreements, all misunderstandings fall away the moment that the spirit has become noble. It is the sign of the noble spirit to comprehend all things, to assimilate all things, to tolerate and to forgive. A flower proves to be genuine by its fragrance; a jewel proves to be genuine by its radiance; a fruit proves to be genuine by its sweetness; a person proves to be genuine by the beauty and sincerity of personality.

When Jesus Christ said, "Blessed are the poor in spirit," that message revealed the true secret of the art of personality, understood in that context as being the effacement of one's own ego. It is the ego of others that disturbs one the most; therefore, as a service to others one willingly chooses to efface one's own ego. The words 'poor in spirit' illustrate the softening of the ego, which then may show a certain charm. This same charm is also seen in persons who have experienced suffering and disappointment, but the true virtue in the softening of the ego lies in one's own initiative taken on the path of self-denial.

It is the gratification of ego that builds up its strength, and the more the satisfaction acquired, the greater is the desire. In this way, one becomes enslaved by one's own ego, although being of Divine origin. Really speaking, one should act as king or queen in one's own kingdom. Otherwise, one falls from sovereignty to slavery, becoming finally a burden to others as well as to oneself.

The great battle that the wise fight is a battle with the self, whereas an egoistic person fights with the ego of others, where the victory can only be temporary. The victory of the wise is permanent, although life's trials become that much harder to endure. On the other hand, when digging deep within the limitations of the self, one might perhaps discover the treasure of the true self.

The training of ego does not necessarily require a life of renunciation, but it is rather a test of balance and of wisdom. Such a training implies the understanding of the reason behind a desire, of what might be the consequences of obtaining satisfaction, of whether or not one can afford the necessary price, and of whether it is a righteous or an unjust desire. Under the spell of a desire, one's awareness of justice, logic and duty is dulled by the grip of ego, and in that state of mind one judges according to one's perceived best interests, one reasons from the point of view of selfishness, and one's feelings of duty are darkened by one's all-pervading image of self.

No doubt, it is difficult to discriminate between right and wrong, between that which is natural and that which is not, between that which is really necessary and that which is not, between that which brings happiness and that which leaves sorrow, but here again the answer is found in the training of ego, by which one comes to realize that one's worst enemy as well as one's best friend, which is wisdom, are both within oneself.

Self consciousness displays endless facets, some reflecting inferiority complexes such as the need for praise and admiration, and others showing superiority complexes such as finding satisfaction in humiliating and dominating others with an unquenchable thirst for self-assertion. The more one tries to dissimulate one's weakness behind a mask of assertion, the more one's self-confidence collapses like a sand castle under the waves of the rising sea, whereas when the ego is softened, it harmonizes in all circumstances like the little bubbles that float upon the waves, even in a stormy sea.

Life can be pictured as a building with doors smaller than one's own size. At every attempt to enter, one knocks one's head against the doorframe, leaving no other device than bending the head when passing through the door. Modesty is not necessarily weakness, nor is it the same as humility, if that is founded upon self-pity. Modesty is a feeling that rises from the living heart, which is secretly conscious of its inner beauty while at the same time veiling itself even from its own sight.

The Hindu word for religion, dharma, meaning duty, could also be understood as consciousness of one's most noble obligations. When attuned to the deep meaning of this interpretation of religion, one realizes that to be religious means to accomplish those duties that have been entrusted to us by destiny as the purpose of our lives. Therefore, it is one's most religious duty to practice the art of personality, so that one might some day become a living example of that ideal, while dancing the sacred dance at the court of Indra, the temple of Divine Presence found within our heart.

11

The Crystallization of the 'All-Pervading'

(Inspired by the Soul Whence and Whither by Hazrat Inayat Khan)

From the 'Absolute', a spark of consciousness sprang forth, and out of this miracle arose individual rays of consciousness, as referred to in the ancient Greek traditions by the term 'logos.'

Individualized consciousness then became concentrated as a centralized point of light, radiating against the darkness. These two opposites developed into a responsive system, following the universal principle of expansion and contraction, which is the fundamental law of all motion, interpreted by the mystics as the breath of God. The Sufis term these two opposite motions "Uruj," meaning expansion and "Nasul", meaning contraction. In this process could be seen the original secret of Time.

In the further process of manifestation every step resulted in various shapes and substances born of the involution of spirit, a path travelled at a later stage in the opposite direction by the evolution of matter. In their structure, these various shapes and substances developed in different proportions of basic elements, such as earth, water, fire, and ether. From these elementary substances developed the mineral, vegetable and animal kingdoms, followed by the creation of the human being.

The soul, pictured in its purest form as a ray of divine light, could be understood as an individualized energy that roams within a sphere where there is neither beginning nor end, neither past nor future, where there is no condition and no object, where the 'I' has no meaning, and where all relative conceptions such as good and bad, happiness and sorrow, and gain and loss have no application. In this state, the soul wanders freely in an enfoldment of everlasting light, which, for human comprehension, has been named the 'angelic spheres'.

Those whose hearts are tuned to the pitch of the 'angelic spheres' will show on earth the most loving qualities. Those who show signs of intelligence have obviously inherited that gift from the 'jinn spheres' (related to the Sanskrit word *jnana*, meaning the power of thought), where the soul, now perfectly conscious of the 'I' concept, as shown, for example, in the desire to be, becomes more captive. Then, in the human state of being the soul is attracted by all definable aspects of manifestation, such as coordinated thoughts under the management of the thinking power, as well as by the heartfelt emotions. Here the body is motivated by action, the mind accumulates experiences, and the heart is the clear mirror which reflects back upon the soul all impressions, without in any way modifying the brightness of the soul's light.

A child born on earth possesses the characteristics which it may have inherited from the parents and ancestors, but at the same time the child possesses other qualities, some of which might be quite foreign to the parents, thus from the beginning of its life showing evidence of affinities to that which it has not yet experienced. One finds among artists, poets, musicians, thinkers, and creators of all types traces of a genius disposition, which might have been absorbed as remnants of impressions experienced prior to the human state of consciousness.

The earthly body is comparable to a lump of clay which has been kneaded thousands and thousands of times over, becoming more and more functional and more and more able to co-ordinate thought, feeling and action, following the evolution of the mineral and the vegetable kingdoms, before finally adopting the human image. It has evolved from the densest possible condition into a living being through the process of the incoming breath, which is the basic secret of life on earth.

All experiences received through the five senses are accumulated in the mind and kept in the memory through the power of breath, which is behind all action and is that energy which keeps the entire mechanism in running order. It is a current that works as a co-coordinating power, assembling together action, thought and feeling in one and the same individual being.

The physical body can also be considered as a universe in itself, and it bears traces of all conditions through which the original lump of clay has passed on its journey through time and space. This explains why one can trace the qualities of mineral kingdom in a rigid-minded person; in a supple-minded person one can trace the qualities of vegetable kingdom, whereas the qualities of the animal kingdom can be traced in a person's uncontrolled passions and fears.

One can intensify either the material aspect or the spiritual aspect of one's being, but again, what is matter? Is it not crystallized spirit?

These two polarities are recognizable in the allegorical concepts of heaven and hell. The idea of heaven and hell exists in some form or other in all religions, permitting religion the determination of what is good and what is evil, and thus providing a great hold upon the masses.

The early scriptures were given at a time when mankind was only seeking for the fulfilment of basic wants, without attaching much importance to concepts such as morality, justice or individual human rights. This explains why heaven was promised to the good doers and the evil-doers were warned of the fires of hell. In fact there is a heaven and a hell for each person, and what is more, the heaven of one person may be hell for another. There is no such thing as an enclosure called heaven where the virtuous ones are welcomed with rewards, nor is there an enclosure called hell where all the wrong-doers are kept in a state of captivity; every person creates his own heaven or hell, and what is more, one might create one's own heaven one day, and one's own hell the next.

On its return journey, the soul passes through the same planes and states through which it travelled on its way to manifestation, taking with it all the impressions that were acquired during life on earth, which constitute the garb of its individuality, until it finally frees itself from all that causes the consciousness of duality, at which point, like a ray of sunlight, it de-personifies itself within the unconditional absolute, or in other words, the divine spirit. All that the soul has borrowed through manifestation is returned to its origin.

Life, which is omnipresent and all-pervading, divides itself in innumerable rays of light as it proceeds towards manifestation, in the same way that light divides itself when it projects its rays upon darkness, and although this process has no apparent purpose, yet in this mystery lies the purpose of all purposes. The outcome of the whole manifestation is to be found in the secret of knowledge; therefore knowledge can be called the purpose of creation. It is knowledge that mystics call self-realization or God-consciousness.

In this connection, Hazrat Inayat Khan says, "The whole of manifestation is just like a tree sprung forth out of a divine root. Nature is like the stem, and all the aspects of nature are like the branches, the leaves, the fruit, the flowers; and from this tree again the same seed is produced, the human soul, which was the first cause of the tree."

Divine origin is seen in the aristocracy of the soul, whereas democracy is born out of the illusion of duality; yet from a mystical point of view, both ends are destined to meet in one and the same ideal: manifestation of the Divine heritage in human nobleness of spirit. A flower proves to be genuine by its fragrance; a jewel proves to be genuine by its radiance; a fruit proves to be genuine by its sweetness; a soul proves to be genuine by the art of harmonizing an aristocratic origin and a democratic spirit. It is a manner that springs forth as a Divine blossom, revealing thereby the reality of the Divine origin.

12

Sufi Tenets

The Message of all times, which is sounding again in this century, reminds mankind that highly respected religious traditions now face the reality of new visions of the pearls contained in all religious symbolism, which are so often hidden under many layers of disguise, pretense, and fanatical thinking, whereas those pearls can only be seen within one's own heart, which, to the mystic, is the real living altar.

As we march courageously onward through the darkness of human ignorance, steadfastly displaying the banner of Spiritual Liberty, we may perhaps discover that Truth can be interpreted as an invitation to become living examples of love, harmony and beauty, communicated on the level of each other's understanding. But Truth is only Truth when not pretending to oneself nor to others about one's own wisdom, but when offering a silent example of an awakening to the everlasting riddle: Who, What, Why, Which, When, Whence and Whither?

The word Sufi means 'wisdom' according to Greek etymology and 'purity' according to Arabic etymology. However, both concepts clearly suggest one and the same ideal. Wisdom is only there when the mind is purified from preconceived ideas, the burdens of dogma and an unrestful conscience. As to the origin of Sufism, one could say that it is just as ancient as the concepts of wisdom and purity, which have always been the inspiration of devotional worship all down the ages. Sufism is not a cult nor is it a school of theology. Sufism is an 'open door,' an attitude of truest sympathy towards all beliefs. Sufism is the essence of all religious ideals and as such, it has even been appropriated by large cultural and religious streams during different periods in history, without ever losing its own identity.

When pronouncing the word Sufism, the 'ism' has a tendency to confine the understanding of wisdom, which is beyond limitations and could never be identified with only one belief, for there are as many descriptions of wisdom as there are seekers on the path. Wisdom might be recognizable, but it is neither tangible nor definable. Therefore, for the one who is really wise, there is only one wisdom, beyond all descriptions and interpretations.

As soon as one attempts to define abstract concepts, one is taken away into the labyrinth of one's own thoughts, which descend into speculations so that one builds up illusions that are then added to the many that one picks up, together with the numerous impressions and influences which constitute our mind world. Then, when one attempts to put one's beliefs and understandings into words, these tend to deviate from the original ideas, and the result of all this is so often presented as being the one and only truth.

For a Sufi, God is not only a heavenly ideal, but also a Friend, a Beloved, with whom one's dealings are as with Lover and Beloved. This explains why all praise is offered to God in thought of the wonders of Creation; and when dealing with one's fellow humans, all actions of kindness and consideration are offered as though to God. However, the wise take care not to pride themselves upon their good deeds, keeping in mind that vanity hides as a veil the presence of God from witin; whereas love for God in the absence of the self results in the expansion of the heart, in the light whereof every action becomes a virtue.

If God is love and if love is sacred, one avoids degrading the value of that sacredness through vain utterances. Once a spark has been kindled, love is in itself a revelation for which no study, no concentration, no meditation and no piety is required. To seek for spirituality without love is a vain search because if spirituality is to be found anywhere it is in the heart, once that kindling spark has grown into a glowing flame, throwing light upon the path once darkened by the shadow of the false ego.

Under the fascination of worldly power, one overlooks the greatness of those inner powers that can be discovered when 'I' is replaced by 'Thou art', while at the same time respecting one's duties toward the accomplishment of the purpose of one's life. This explains why one of the great ideals of the Sufi is the awakening of a broader outlook, with deeper understanding for the tragic misunderstandings that divide the earnest followers of various cultural traditions.

All religions are, in their origin, of Divine inspiration, but like the image of clear water poured into different coloured glasses, as soon as Divine inspiration is contained in human thought, it acquires the image of one's thinking. We then call one religion Hinduism and another Buddhism, while others are called Judaism, Christianity or Islam, as well as many other religious denominations, known or unknown to the world at large.

A Sufi is a religious soul whose nature is to be free from imposed theories, and who is perfectly conscious that life is not necessarily just what one might think it to be. Life is not only lived at the level of physical experience, nor only at the levels of thought and feeling, but also, and most importantly, at a still higher level of consciousness, where the self is no more a barrier separating reality from illusion. At this level of consciousness there are neither limitations nor opposites, and there is no relationship with speculative references to the dualistic concept of Divinity. When trying to explain God one only fashions an individual concept, limited to the size of one's own mind world.

Another subject found in Sufi teachings is the alchemy of happiness, which, as we know from fairy tales, is the use of a magic formula to turn metal into gold. This mystical legend symbolizes so beautifully the basic principle of the Inner School of the Sufis, where deep consideration is offered to the importance of training the ego upon a thorny path known as the art of personality, where false identification and illusory aspirations cease to be a hindrance to the discovery of the Divine presence hidden as a pearl in one's heart. This requires constant efforts to forge the character into a living example of wisdom, so as to become a bringer of happiness to brothers and sisters of all beliefs.

Hazrat Inayat Khan came to us with a message of 'Spiritual Liberty', revealing thereby the real nature of spirituality as being inherent to the liberty of thought and feeling.

Another great teaching of our Master is 'the Unity of Religious Ideals', which implies being liberated from such feelings as 'my religion' and 'your religion'. True religion is the religion of heart, and since there are many hearts, there are just as many religious ideals springing forth from one and the same source, once the doors of the Temple of the heart are open, placing one face to face with the living God within.

The message of Love, Harmony and Beauty is like a stream flowing onwards through our daily lives, and this current of purity and wisdom is the true essence of that which is understood by the term Sufi.

13

The Science Called Pranayama

The science called Pranayama was originally formulated by sage Patanjali and later became the main subject of what is called Raja yoga, known to the yogis for centuries. It is a path of wisdom that flourished at its highest in the time of Sri Ramakrishna Paramahansa who was the great teacher of two of the most well known Raja yoga specialists, namely Swami Vivekananda and Ramana Maharshi.

The basic principles of this science are the awakening of the Kundalini energy as well as control over the technique of conducting that energy to a chosen goal, thereby becoming conscious of the brilliant light that shines as an aura about each chakra, in proportion to the luminosity of the Prana flow.

This process can be explained as follows: when focusing one's thought on a chosen chakra, that chakra resonates to the vibrations of one's thought, in attunement with an invisible Prana flow which links the thought to that chakra. At that moment the source of the Kundalini energy, which is dormant at the base of the spine, awakens in accordance with the intensity of the thought, creating an impact on the chakra at which point the initial thought-flow and the Kundalini energy both meet, like a completed circuit joining two wires of opposite polarity.

It is important to understand that when a chosen chakra has been awakened, all other chakras simultaneously react to that process, although their awakening is of a finer degree of intensity. When considering this very important point, it is obvious that great care should be taken in the choice of the chakra that one decides to awaken for a given purpose.

For instance, when prasticing the Zikar, the heart chakra is awakening and the consciousness becomes thereby most brilliant, while at the same time the other chakras awaken accordingly, although with lesser intensity.

When awakening the chakras that influence the physical impulses, one certainly becomes most charismatic, whereas the other chakras, which have also awakened, although to a lesser degree, do not necessarily shine accordingly, seen from a spiritual point of view.

There is also a reverse technique, which is also practised according to ancient yoga science, that consists of awakening the Kundalini stream without focusing it upon a chosen chakra. Eventually the shining light of the awakened Kundalini stream shall then project its brightness upon all chakras in turn, following a natural sequence. This meditation is only done in a complete isolation from daily activities.

The science of breath, seen from a spiritual point of view does not necessarily mean development of volume, but it refers essentially to refinement of the inhalation as well as to the ability to direct the breath mentally to a chosen imaginary image. This development is of essential importance for a growing physical well being, as well as providing the support for higher consciousness.

One aspect of the power of breath is revealed in its special function of absorbing from the cosmos subtle vibrations along the breath-web-pathways, called Nadis. In this process, called Swara yoga, the influence of the earth element inspires steadiness; the water element motivates progress; the fire element creates excitement; the air element offers receptivity; and the ether element inspires spiritual attunement.

Breath can be disciplined in various ways. In all cases the idea is for the breath to adopt various rhythmic patterns, as well as to focus upon various mentally traced images and concepts of specific characteristics. Once this technique has been practised, the next step leads to the appropriate adaptation of the power of breath to all circumstances in one's daily life. This of course implies making a wise use of the different qualities of breath.

a. When the positive energy (Purusha) of the breath manifests more pronouncedly during exhalation through the right nostril, this favours physical, mental or emotional modes of expression (Jelal).

b. When the receptive energy (Prakriti) manifests more pronouncedly during the exhalation through the left nostril, this favours a perceptive and receptive disposition (Jemal).

c. When positive and receptive energy manifest simultaneously through the breath, this is creative of a Kemal condition, either in an exciting situation resulting from a clash of opposite energies, or in an elevating meditative condition when these opposite energies are consciously brought into balance through peaceful attunement.

Science is now discovering more and more that the breath, when active either through the left nostril or the right has a corresponding influence on the brain itself. Pranayama, the science of breath, teaches the ability to direct the breath either to the right or to the left, awakening thereby either active or responsive dispositions known to the Sufis as Jelal or Jemal, which clearly have specific influences in our daily life.

14

Prana, the Mystical Power of Breath

There is no darkness. Life is light, omnipotent and omnipresent. When dispersed, light appears dim or dark, but when concentrated it becomes bright. It is only the contrast between concentrated and scattered light that accounts for the whole scenery of creation. For instance, when gathered, light manifests as luminosity, and when scattered, it appears as movement. On the level of creation, one might say that the heart, mind and body are different grades of radiance localized within the limitations of feelings, thoughts and forms.

The human being is so constituted that by the help of the sense organs and the stimulus of light and sound, one becomes aware of all that is around one. Light and sound open the channels of communication, as for example, when the voice penetrates through the hearing to the mind and, on a subtle level of consciousness, even as far as the heart of the listener.

Just as there may be a piece of land which has lain waste and barren for want of water or sunlight, so faculties which have hitherto remained slumbering, may be awakened when nourished by the mystical power of the breath.

The breath has the tendency to extend outwards, but the further it spreads, the fainter becomes its magnetism, just as light diminishes in luminosity at a distance and by comparison might be termed darkness, although in reality it is only a lesser degree of light, which again becomes brighter as one turns back toward the source of radiance. Breath, like light, can have an influence on others, and its magnetic intensity varies according to its radiance within the inner depths of the true self. The breath is the vehicle upon which the consciousness rides out into the world during exhalation. Upon inhalation the consciousness becomes loaded with impressions that transit the mechanism of the five senses before reaching the coordinating centers of the mind, where these finally become intelligible. Therefore the breath is like a bridge, connecting the outer world with the inner world, wherein dwells the true self, the consciousness, the spectator of all impressions received through the five senses.

By the practice of Shagal, one withdraws the magnetism of breath from one direction and projects it in another direction, meaning that instead of the breath being dispersed outwardly one directs it inwardly. The magnetism of breath, also called Prana, is then revealed as light and sound. In the Vedanta, breath is called Suran or Swara, meaning 'sound'. This practice wakens awareness of energy with two opposite directions, one that draws inward, and one that reaches outward from within.

When closing the hearing, one listens to the unstruck sound of the cosmos, audible within as 'Hu'. When closing the sight, one searches for the inner light, revealed as luminosity unrelated to any material brilliancy. When closing off the taste, one replaces it by a savoring of values unknown to the tongue, which are spiritually related to the ecstasy felt in the power of silence. When closing the nostrils and blocking the incoming flow of Prana, one veils the self-consciousness, retaining the Prana energy within, which, in the absence of the self, is now revealed in the Divine fragrance of the abstract spheres. The fifth sense, the touch, is sublimated to a higher level of perception.

When blocking the five senses one pulls a veil over the outer impressions in an effort to open contact with the consciousness within, and the working of the senses is reversed. That is to say, one draws from within instead of from without, and one then discovers the hidden source of all sensorial energy, whereas the mind inevitably distorts outer perceptions in giving them an identity. When closing the senses to all incoming impressions, one finds oneself face to face with an open window upon the innermost depth of one's own being.

The Sufi practice of Shagal is the parallel of Hindu yoga practice called Mudra yoga. The 'Antarajnani' or knower of the unformed world within sees the light with closed eyes, hears the inner sound called 'Anahad' or 'Saut-e-sarmad' with closed ears and experiences all the other inner sensations while directing the breath inwardly. The first stage is called 'Sultani Nasurah', and further steps are known as 'Sultani Mahmud' and 'Sultani Kaskar'.

15

Injustice in Justice

To human understanding, justice means returning good for good and bad for bad according to basic legal principles, whereas seen from another angle the concept of justification is obviously limited to personal experiences interpreted according to the conflicting influences of one's surroundings and pre-conceived ideas, which result either in destructive motives or unjustified infatuations with persons or concepts, producing that which one is persuaded in one's own opinion if right or wrong.

When confronted by such calamities of nature as tornados, floods, earthquakes and volcanic eruptions and the disastrous consequences thereby encountered, the human understanding of the concept of justice is seriously challenged; and again, when seeing the cruelties perpetuated in the animal world, where some creatures are given life with the necessity to kill so that may survive, whereas others are destined to be offered as nourishment to the stronger ones, it is then that one's faith regarding any concept of justice is completely shattered, and one is left wondering where Divine compassion could ever be found.

Obviously, the human understanding of justice cannot, in truth, follow the lines of the Creator's logic, but it might seek a compromise way out of the paradoxical laws of creation which constantly baffle the human and animal realms, because that is the way that destiny has chosen to proclaim its all-pervading magnificence.

Seen from another perspective, Nature's characteristics offer quite a different picture, as far as its contestable signs of compassion reach, and where it does appear to be compassionate, for example, resulting in the gift of natural instinct to the animal kingdom. To human kind, free will has been bestowed, allowing the ability to wisely maneuver along lines of individual judgement with determination, but these qualities could never be of any use to others with the warmth of the heart toward those in need.

If absolute justice—according to one's personal understating—cannot be found in nature nor in humanity nor in the animal worlds, one might perhaps venture to discover one's own responsibility to help others overcome the detrimental effects of injustice experienced at all levels of creation, as opposed to maintaining illusionary justifications of Divine compassion as variously understood from the human point of view.

Human compassion is expressed with sympathetic understanding and love, without expecting anything in return. But again, love is perhaps only found at a deeper level in one person than in another, just as water is discovered at different depths beneath the earth, and is either clear or muddy according to the condition of the soil; likewise, human understanding is either cloudy or bright in accordance with the condition of the heart. Furthermore, just as water makes the earth fertile, in the same way the magic of love makes the heart abundantly compassionate, and every impulse that arises, sooner or later bears sweet and fragrant fruits. It is then that Divine compassion can be found, concealed as a pearl is hidden in a shell, and blessed are those who have the privilege of discovering that precious jewel, which is nevertheless the inheritance of every soul.

16

Concentration

When following a project, one develops more and more will-power, with which one is able to maintain the realization of that project. While concentrating one is not conscious of the power of will involved, but sooner or later, whatever one concentrates upon becomes an intoxication unless one is prepared to liberate oneself from the domination of the project in mind.

An impression is the shadow of external circumstances received through the five senses and traced automatically upon the screen of the mind, while will power is the energy which motivates the thought, enabling thereby a coordination of colours, shapes and lines, creating thereby an intelligible image.

Everything which is perceived through the five senses is stored deep down in the memory in a scattered form when not actively called upon. However, when wanted, all the pieces are again correctly re-assembled, reconstructing thereby the original image. This situation experienced when awake, differs from dreams, where the light of intelligence is on standby, and the power of the will is slumbering, the regrouping of the thought-pieces lacks complete coordination, which explains the unreality of dream images. The difference between dream and imagination is that during sleep it is called 'dream', whereas in a wakened state it is called 'imagination'.

Concentration fixes the impressions received and also helps secure the retention of thought, which obviously explains why memory is so dependent upon the correct observation of an image, as it also is dependent upon will power with regard to the creation of thought. And what is more, besides the impressions received through the five senses, there are much finer ones which vibrate within the feeling heart and, as a magnet can hold pieces of metal by the power of attraction, in the same way, thoughts may be steadily fixed in the concentrated mind by the magnetic power of the feeling heart.

Concentration may create positive or negative results either intentionally or unintentionally according to whether the concentration is willingly directed, or whether one is obsessed by one's own thinking. Obviously, if one is not able to delete unwanted thoughts, there is some danger of becoming a slave to the power of concentration. For this reason both holding and erasing, the two great applications of concentration, should be developed simultaneously.

The holding of a thought is constructive inasmuch as it helps bring about inner strength and steadiness of mind, whereas the other power, the ability to delete unwanted entangled thoughts, helps free the mind of worries and fears, and could be called de-concentration.

Besides inspiring images, the most uplifting subject of concentration may be found in the personalities of spiritual souls whom one idealizes and whose examples offer either creative or spiritual guidance. Whatever be the chosen ideal, it is the intensity of one's devotion that shall effect the beauty of the achievement.

When opening one's heart to God, finding oneself face to face with the Divine presence, at that very moment of self-redemption one realizes that what one thought to be oneself, was only an illusion, yet paradoxically individual consciousness is at the same time God's consciousness, like the drop of sea water which is just a drop and yet at the same time is the sea itself in an individualized form.

17

Contemplation

When following an idea, one may be fascinated by it, but when giving it up for a better cause, the will power is thereby strengthened, which is the fruit of conviction assisted by wisdom. This is what could be understood by the term 'contemplation.'

While contemplating an idea without the guidance of wisdom one might become intoxicated with the chosen concept, which could then degenerate into a fixed idea or a preconception.

In other words, whatever one contemplates upon, sooner or later produces a significant effect with either positive or negative consequences; one can either become elevated, or if one is not prepared to liberate oneself from self-illusion, one can become intoxicated.

An impression is the shadow of external circumstances received through the five senses and traced automatically upon the screen of the mind, whereas will power is the light which illuminates the scenario of the thought, enabling thereby a creative coordination of shapes, lines and colours as an intelligible image.

Everything that is perceived through the five senses is stored, scattered deep down in the memory when not actively called upon. However, when wanted, all the pieces are again assembled, reconstructing thereby the original image.

This differs from the dream, when the light of intelligence is in a standby condition and the power of the will is slumbering. In this condition, the regrouping of many thought-pieces lacks coordination, which explains the complete lack of logic in dreams.

Then again, the apparent difference between dream and imagination is that during sleep the slumbering thought is called a 'dream', whereas in a wakened state the contemplative thought is called 'imagination'.

Contemplation fixes impressions received, securing their retention within the thought patterns, which obviously explains why memory is so dependent upon the correct observation of an image, as it is also dependent upon will power with regard to the creation of thought.

Besides the impressions received through the five senses, there are also much finer ones which vibrate within the feeling heart and, as a magnet can hold pieces of metal by the power of attraction, in the same way, thoughts may be steadily fixed in the mind by the magnetic power of the feeling heart.

As said, contemplation may have positive or negative consequences; therefore, if one is not able to delete unwanted thoughts, there is some risk in becoming a slave to the power of thought. For this reason both holding and erasing should be developed simultaneously.

The holding of a thought is constructive insofar as it helps bring about inner strength and steadiness of mind, whereas the ability to delete entangled thoughts, which could be called de-concentration, helps free the mind of worries and fears.

The most uplifting subject of contemplation may be found in the personalities of spiritual souls whom one idealizes and whose examples indirectly offer spiritual guidance, but whatever be the chosen ideal, it is mainly the intensity of one's devotion that shall effect the beauty of the guidance.

When finding oneself face to face with the Divine presence, at that very moment of self-redemption one realizes that what one thought about oneself was only an illusion, yet paradoxically individual consciousness is at the same time Divine consciousness, like the drop of sea water which is just a drop, and yet at the same time is the sea itself in an individualized entity.

18

Five Approaches to the Mysticism of Sound

From the Angle of Visible and Audible Vibrations

Life, from which all seen and unseen manifestations of creation originate, is in itself silent and invisible, whereas all of life's creation is mostly audible or visible in an infinite variety of manifestations. The mystery of the whole universe resides in the fact that these manifestations could also be understood as being spaces within the space, and it is within these spaces, also called 'akashas', that the cosmic energy manifests in different shades of colour, as well as in tones of sound, vibrating from the very lowest to the very highest pitch within the all pervading space.

Sound and colour are perceived through the channels of the two senses of hearing and sight, where appropriate faculties are motivated, as well as through the three other, indirectly related faculties of taste, touch, and the olfactory ability, all of which together are the expression of what could be described as centralized consciousness, or the root of all senses, where all faculties are fundamentally coordinated.

The dull sound of the vibrations of the Earth element, which cause the surface to rumble and resonate, and whose characteristic is solidity, also manifest in various shades ranging from brown to golden yellow. These hollow sounds have the quality of motivating the need to communicate.

The sound of the vibrations of water element varies in accordance with circumstances, as the water flows onwards, overcoming all obstacles with a clarifying effect. The water element reveals itself in a variety of green shades, related to the environment and to substances entering into the element. The characteristic of water element is fluidity.

The highly-strung vibrations of fire element, which have the characteristic of brilliancy, are seen in shades of red. These specific vibrations awaken and encourage physical and psychological impulses.

The vibrations of air element, which reach beyond the concept of audible sound and visible colour, could nevertheless be pictured in various shades of blue. These vibrations, with the characteristic of expansiveness, are most appropriate sources of inspiration.

The everlasting sound and the ever-present brilliant light of ether element, which is the life-giver of all other elements, are imperceptible to human senses but might be awakened in one's consciousness as brilliancy, as all-pervading sound and as unlimited expansion, as those vibrations are known to the mystics.

From the Angle of Motion and Rhythm

Motion, which is the characteristic of life itself, serves as a bridge between the abstract nature of the cosmos and human consciousness, and the root of all creation is to be found in the mystery of all-pervading vibrations motivated by one single energy, which unfold in an infinite variety, giving rise, of course, to all sound.

The nature of motion is rhythm, and the entire universe works according to the laws of rhythm. This is seen in the waxing and waning of the moon, the changing of seasons, the ebb and flow of the tides, and the sunrise and sunset. The rhythmic pulse can certainly be heard in the crashing of the waves, in the gentle fluttering of the leaves, in the songs of birds, and in many other sounds of nature. The motive energy of the sun and the Prana energy in the air as well as the attractive forces of the earth and water and other elements, all have specific effects upon the conditions of life.

From the Angle of the Music of East and West

Music, where human creative ability encounters inspiration, teaches one to listen and to perceive a concept that cannot be defined within the realm of the spoken word, but rather at the level of imagination, where immaterial shapes and shades enrich one's thoughts and feelings.

The magic of human voice resides in the power of breath, which communicates to the heart of the listener the subtle vibrations of the 'mysticism of sound' through the Prana flow. The magic of a musical instrument resides in its ability to translate the technical command of the player into tones adapted to the cultural traditions of east and west, varying in numerous ways through the ages.

Music is music, whether in the east or in the west, because all music comes from one and the same source of inspiration. Nevertheless, some specific differences could be described. Western music is mainly polyphonic, and is structured according to modulating scale patterns, sustained by chords placed vertically to accompany the melodic lines, all of which creates harmonic systems; whereas eastern music is mainly monophonic and non-modulative, accompanied mostly by rhythmic patterns called Talas, and sustained by accompanying instruments holding continuous basic tones. Eastern music also consists of a great number of specific sets of grouped tonal intervals called Ragas, upon which melodic improvisations are elaborated without any alterations in the interval groupings.

The mystery of the mysticism of sound could be recognized in its power to affect the physical, mental and sentimental conditions of the listener, whether experienced as religious music, military music, joyful music, dance music, peaceful music, uplifting music or meditative music.

From a Philosophical Angle

There is a great mystery in the magical power of sound and its diverse effects upon humans and animals, as well as upon nature in its unfoldment throughout all levels of evolution. Some of the impacts of sound are a consequence of repetitions of rhythmic patterns, adjusted to either even or uneven rhythmic beats. Other effects produced by sound, ranging from the lowest to the highest audible ones perceived by the human ears, awaken subtle reactions within the cells of the inner ear, highlighting certain chakras in various ways of which one may or may not be conscious. The dynamics, or changes between soft and loud, and the resonance of the overtones also have great influence upon the psychic and physical conditions.

Specific moods are generated through the mystical power of sound, awakening the Jelal, the Jemal, or the Kemal rhythms of the breath. This explains why certain rhythmic patterns, such as those found in military music, for instance, induce the body to march forward, while others invite the body to accommodate a partner in the graceful movements of a dance. Still others again bring the entire physical and psychic conditions into a state of excitement and turmoil, or into a state of peace, depending upon the attunement.

Music can also be descriptive of inspiring scenes, as in symphonic poems, folkloric melodies and religious ceremonies of all types. These melodic enchantments have the power to motivate one's imagination, both when heard and when recreated in memory. The magic effect of music can certainly be confirmed by those who have received from music the gift of hope during great sadness, by those who have found therein temporary consolation in the midst of an unsatisfied and never-ending longing, or by those who have received from music an unfoldment of happiness.

If the mysticism of sound could be recognised in any realistic format, it could perhaps be found in the art of creating a specific atmosphere capable of dragging one's attention away from oneself, and redirecting that attention to other realms of consciousness.

From the Angle of the Mystic

For the mystic, there is a higher level of music, which is discovered when awakening to the all-pervading sound 'Hu' in the cosmos.

The mysticism of sound can be best understood as the secret source of all inspiration, silently heard within the temple of the heart, the true abode of all human consciousness, and when the 'I' concept is replaced by a modest call to the Divine beloved within, one then realizes the reality of the all-pervading, unknown Infinity. This can be glimpsed in profoundly heart-breaking folkloric melodies, and may very well be experienced in the magic atmosphere of the Singing Zikar.

Mysticism could best be described as the secret essence or the perfume of knowledge. If knowledge is not within our reach, we may nevertheless distinguish the perfume of that flower.

Mysticism of all ages has been known in different ways, having been referred to in so many folkloric fables and fairytales, which relate it to strange powers and miracles, but mysticism cannot be defined in words, in doctrines, in theories or in philosophical statements; it can only be recognized by a mystical mind, which explains why it has been diversely misunderstood and misinterpreted.

What brings still more confusion regarding mysticism is that there are endless numbers of so-called mystics, occultists, spiritualists, fortune tellers and parapsychologists, sometimes calling themselves by such names as 'Christian mystics,' or 'Jewish mystics' or 'Muslim mystics.' Mysticism cannot represent different sects or cults or belong to any particular religion or belief. There is no such thing as 'this' mysticism or 'that' mysticism, or 'my' mysticism or 'your' mysticism. There is only mysticism, which is neither this nor that, neither yours nor mine. There are numberless seekers after truth who have devoted years of their lives in vain to the search for mysticism, but who have returned empty-handed because one does not search for mysticism; mysticism searches after the seeker.

If the mystic has religious tendencies, these are out of love for the God Ideal, and not from regard for rules, regulations, principles or dogmas. The mystic makes intelligible the laws of the seen and the unseen worlds, knowing that nothing can bring more intense happiness than belief can, but it can only suffice our needs inasmuch as we are in harmony with our self and with others. Unfortunately, for those who stick to 'I am' and 'God is', emphasizing the opposing poles of duality, belief becomes a self-created entity rather than a humble recognition of the Divine reality.

The mystic waves the 'magic wand', turning disbelief into belief, where both logic and illogic are intermingled within the world of imagination, and then again turning imagination into reality. This all seems out of reach, but for the mystic, who thinks and feels at a completely different pitch, it seems so natural. Nevertheless, the mystic always hides abstract concepts from simple eyes, knowing that those who think they see do not always know, and those who really know do not always say. In this connection, it is obvious that however much one studies metaphysics, philosophy, and all types of analysis, although these are all precious contributions to the storehouse of our intellect, there is still another world of knowledge to be discovered. If our life has any purpose, it is the raising of consciousness, and not the mere enrichment of knowledge.

This concept might appear to some as plain pride, but in fact pride is not pride when it is pride in God. The consciousness of God, which is our true self, becomes the false assertion of oneself as soon as the concept of duality is in the picture. Therefore, when pride in God is offered in a truly sacred manner, as nothingness at the feet of the All-Pervading, it becomes the highest possible form of worship, and at the same time the truest and sincerest form of humility.

The goal of the God-ideal might appear to be an intensification of consciousness of self, whereas in fact it is the loss of the 'self' concept, dissolved into the concept of 'God'. In this process, the false self, or in other words what we imagine to be ourselves, is lost, and what is gained is the consciousness of the true self, which is God alone. This process is what is understood by traversing the path to the 'God-ideal.'

When the mystic arrives at this stage of selflessness, the mystic hears through the ears of God, sees through the eyes of God, works with the hands of God, walks with the feet of God, and the thoughts and feelings are none other than thoughts and feelings of God. There is no longer the concept of duality, of 'I' and 'God.' When understanding this, one is able to see oneself within the Universe, just as well as one sees the Universe within. One is as small as a drop in the Universe, and at the same time, the Universe is as a universe within a drop, and if there is any worship, it is just that: to see God in all, and all in God. At this stage, one stands face to face with truth, beyond all human definitions.

If the mystic has an aim in life, it is to understand God as a reality, and to help mankind discover that the whole of God's creation is created out of love, for the sake of love, and that love is its purpose.

Mysticism is the path of liberation from the captivity of that illusion which arises when one assumes a duality in the concept 'human and divine'.

19

Spirituality

In reality everyone is spiritual, because life itself is spirit, and spirit is life-power, motivating the materialized garb of the self. The self identifies itself with its limited mental and physical status, without realizing that the all-pervading immanence of life is that indescribable power which is constantly manifesting behind all impulses.

Spiritual ideals cannot be the property of one particular transmission because of their universal nature. Spirituality is a call for the human right of thought and feeling on the spiritual path. This call has been sounding ever since eternity but has not always been understood, which explains why various terminologies employed to explain that call generally misinterpret its real meaning. Besides this, what brings still more confusion regarding spirituality is that there are endless numbers of self-proclaimed mystics, occultists, spiritualists, fortunetellers and parapsychologists whose mission seems to be to satisfy those who are chasing after miracles.

There is a well-known theatre play that mentions the famous words "To be or not to be," emphasizing the fact that striving in this difficult life requires one to choose to be. One might assume that this principle also applies to obtaining spirituality, whereas spirituality does not have any meaning unless one discovers that to be spiritual means exactly the reverse of wanting to be something, or pretending to be something; in the case of spirituality, 'not to be is to be.'

Spirituality cannot be limited within doctrines nor defined in words, and it cannot be taught or learned; it can only be discovered by way of the heart. Therefore, spirituality really means rebirth, in the sense that one begins to discover that it has always been one's birthright. Spirituality could best be described as the perfume of true knowledge, although it has been illustrated in all ages in many folkloric fairy-tales, which have given spirituality the appearance of being related to strange powers and eccentric behaviour.

We imagine that to become spiritual means becoming higher and higher, but have we ever stopped to discover that everything that we have wanted to obtain 'up there' is already right here in our own hearts? Spirituality means losing the desire to impress others, whereby one comes unconsciously to identify with the divine presence; otherwise spirituality mostly remains just a dream, if one fails to see that the means to obtain inner realization cannot be the goal; the goal is further still.

Numerous methods are offered in view of discovering the Light of Truth!

There are also thousands of spiritual schools!

But unless one tries to hold the ego under control, one is wasting one's time, and only facing disillusionment. Disillusion in spirituality is even more discouraging than disillusion in worldly affairs.

The ego is like an engine with tremendously powerful energy, but it can only be useful if it is wisely guided in all circumstances. In the same way, the most powerful locomotive would be helpless if there were no rails to roll on, and what is the good of rails without an engine to roll on them? In this context the engine obviously pictures the power of the ego, which is kept under control while rolling along the rails of wisdom.

One cannot get rid of the ego, but one can train it appropriately so that it can be used for beneficial purposes. Let us stop asking, "What can others do for us?" Let us start by asking ourselves, "What can we do for others?"

Before even venturing to tread on the spiritual path, the first step to take is to become a true brother or sister within the limits of one's own conception of good and bad. One then realizes that to be victorious over others does not mean having conquered them, which is in fact an inner defeat. To be defeated is not necessarily to be vanquished; it might be an inner victory, the victory over ego.

The unfoldment of innate nobility inspires one to be conscious of one's responsibilities. All disputes and disagreements fall away the moment the human spirit becomes conscious of its Divine origin, which may be seen in the aristocracy of the human spirit and at the same time the democracy with which one opens one's heart to others.

Spirituality cannot be analyzed because it does not correspond to physical qualities nor to psychological definitions, but is recognizable in a natural tendency toward moral integrity and self-discipline. It is a condition where the feeling heart is constantly activated, unconditionally pouring out inner emotions, which have an uplifting influence upon those who are responsive to the effect of the magnetism of a spiritually awakened soul.

Spirituality means to offer others the fruits of one's experience so that others might be inspired to discover the true light within. The light of the glowing sun is not limited to just one ray. That light shines in an infinite number of rays, cast in all directions. The light of truth is not only reserved for the spiritual seekers. It shines in the hearts of all. Nevertheless, the brilliancy of that light varies in its intensity, dependent upon the transparency of the ego.

20

The Inner Life

When the mind has been purified from the many dogmas, speculations, pre-conceived ideas and doctrines that, all down the ages, have been placed like veils over the phenomena of the Spirit of Guidance, one finally realises that inner guidance has always been present, constantly available insofar as one's attunement to that guidance is awakened. When one then offers to help lift the burden of others' misunderstandings, the language of the heart communicates steadfast sympathy while one helps disperse the illusion of various speculative interpretations of the one and only Truth.

Among the numberless purposes in one's life, one might take for granted that the ideals that secure a balanced condition of body, mind, heart and soul are all those related to Life itself, such as the urge for knowledge and the longing for happiness. As to whether a material ideal could lead to inner realization, one might say that from the point of view of the Divine purpose, even a material ideal could very well be the fulfilment of a spiritual one, because every effort made, whether material or spiritual, brings one consciously or unconsciously nearer to the Ultimate Goal. Each small step made may be seen as a humble contribution to the fulfilment of the Divine purpose, which could be understood as a state of constant formation inspired by a central theme: life in all its infinite variety.

The purpose of life is not only found in rising to the greatest achievements, but also in the widening of the consciousness. No experience in life is worthless; no single moment is really wasted, providing one is wise enough to carefully assemble the bits and pieces of past memories and discover in these as many lessons as may be needed on the path of inner awakening. The self, 'the consciousness', rejoices or suffers unrest from positive or negative thoughts or actions, but when losing sight of itself and focusing all its energy on the Divine Presence, it becomes radiant. The self is only a channel; it is the soul that is ultimately the life within and the spectator of all, and like a mirror, impressions reflected upon the pure surface of the soul leave no trace whatsoever.

The path to inner consciousness is a thorny one, and that consciousness can only said to be truly awakened when one chooses to forge one's character so as not to be a burden to others. This art of personality teaches one that happiness is only there when one strives to offer happiness to others, overlooking all that disturbs one, such as opinions that are not in accordance with one's own thinking. Progress on the path comes in trying to rise above one's own failures, knowing that in every fall there is a hidden stepping stone to success, providing one is willing to attune oneself to the rhythm of all those who cross one's path, and in whom one might eventually discover a hidden spark of guidance.

The inner life is a journey that requires thoughtful planning and constant dedication to avoid an unwanted return to the starting point. Among the obligations that can pull one back during the journey, one, by no means to be underestimated, is the debt owed to those left behind. The fulfilment of one's obligations is not only essential from a material point of view but it is also a most sacred duty on the inner path, and as such it is the first step to be made toward God-consciousness.

The inner life is a path of freedom, that is why every effort is made to free oneself from all those regrets that are a hindrance to progress, regrets such as unfulfilled worldly ambitions, past torments, hatred and an unrestful conscience. The vehicle used during this journey is energy with two wheels—will power and wisdom. Harmonizing these two aspects secures a perfect state of balance at all levels of consciousness: balance of thought and feeling, balance of action and repose, balance of material and spiritual ideals. It is then that the traveller on the path of the inner life is able to offer treasures of thoughtful deeds and uplifting examples of love, harmony and beauty to all those encountered.

The Inner life means making God the very ideal to which one relates, calling God by sacred names evoking such attributes as Judge, Forgiver, Friend and Beloved, as well as numberless other qualifications traditionally adopted by various religions. By this means, belief in God becomes a tangible reality, and the feeling heart turns to the Divine presence for help and guidance. One looks up to God, the Beloved, when one is broken-hearted; one looks up to God, the Helpful Friend, when deprived of sympathy in this cruel world; one looks up to God, the Lord of Justice, when worldly disillusionment has broken one's trust; one looks up to God, the Forgiver, when one is tortured by an unrestful conscience.

The Inner life can be described as the realization of one's nothingness, when the heart becomes empty of the self and at the same time full of the object of one's Ideal. This state remains elusive, though, owing to the constant interference of the ego, which stubbornly tries to bar the way to any progress on the path of inner realization.

The ego constantly puts one to the test when one strives to harmonize oneself with all those conditions in which life places one, such as by communicating with others at their own level of understanding, answering their smiles with a smile, offering tears to their tears, standing side by side with them in their joys and pains, helping them when they stumble over their own self-assertion, and performing conscientiously all those outward roles that are expected from us while experiencing the great tragedies and comedies seen in human nature. Naturally, the one who succeeds in this certainly appears to be a mystery to the average person, who cannot possibly comprehend such selfless behaviour.

However, religious or pious one may be, unless one discovers the reality of a living God alive in one's own heart, one is like a fatherless child. It is therefore that the task on the inner path is to establish a godly relationship in one's life, for in so doing, a new dimension of understanding with God is revealed, ultimately making of oneself a living God. But the one who is God-conscious speaks little about the inner life, whereas the self-centered displays all doubts and fears in endless arguments, debates and assertions.

Although, the traveller on the inner path is clad in 'veils of silence' from respect for the sacredness of the journey, yet the traveller is never alone, because the Divine presence is always present. It is in the awareness of that Presence that one conceives God as Love, Lover and Beloved. As lovers of God, our love reveals to us that we are the beloved ones of God, for we become conscious that we are at the same time human and Divine.

21

Not to Be is to Be

Hazrat Inayat Khan said: "We are all born spiritual because life is spirit."

We are sometimes intrigued, however, by persons thought to be spiritual because of appearance or for some other reason, and spirituality mostly remains a mystery. Nevertheless, as far as we ourselves are concerned, and to be honest with ourselves and others, we could try to make a reality out of that mystery. Perhaps we are already spiritual, but we do not realize it. And if we expect a teacher to make a spiritual person out of us, nothing will ever happen, and we shall end up putting the blame on the teacher.

We all know that striving in this difficult life requires one either to be that which seems desirable, or to suffer the consequences of not being that: in other words, to be or not to be. Therefore, we tend to assume that 'to be' also applies to obtaining spirituality, but spirituality does not have any meaning unless one discovers that it is exactly the reverse of wanting or pretending to be something. Before making the first humble step on the path of spirituality, one must realize that spirituality means losing the desire to be, and thereby unconsciously identifying one's self with spirituality.

Spirituality is the path to happiness, but if for some reason we are not happy, it is very often the result of our own failings. Furthermore, if we want to be happy on our own, it shall not last long. Happiness is only happiness if it is shared, nor can it be acquired at the cost of the sacrifice of others. But in order to be able to offer happiness to others, one must build it up within oneself.

There are numerous methods. There are numerous types of yogas, there are hundreds of spiritual schools, but unless we try to hold the ego under control, we are wasting our time, facing the prospect of disillusion; and disillusion in spirituality is worse than disillusion in worldly affairs.

Spirituality is a challenge to try to improve oneself, as far as one's own conception of good and bad goes; spirituality is not a school where one learns to crush the ego of others. At every step on this path one is reminded that to be victorious does not mean having victory over others, which is in reality an inner defeat, and that to be defeated is not necessarily a loss; it might be an inner victory, the victory over the ego. Paradoxically, though, one can never get rid of the ego; therefore, why not train it appropriately so that it can be used for beneficial purposes? If we did not have an ego, we would not be able to accomplish anything, either good or bad. The most powerful engine is helpless if there are no rails to roll on, and what is the good of rails without an engine to roll upon them? The ego is an engine with tremendously powerful energy that can only be of value if it is kept under control, for material as well as for spiritual experiences.

To be spiritual does not mean flying up in the air. It means developing physical, mental and emotional disciplines. Spirituality is not focused just only in one direction; it is developed in every direction.

As one goes along on the spiritual path, one encounters numerous precious experiences, but as soon as one is tempted to boast about these to others, all those precious accomplishments fall away into dust, although one might have thought that one's level of spirituality was indefinitely secured.

Spirituality is not a speculative adventure. There is no searching after phenomena. Spirituality only means to be a human being, so that others might perhaps benefit from an example, as described by the magic words:

"Not to be is to be!"

22

Poem of the Music Composition

Chanson Exotique

Oh, my captivating ego, conqueror so oft in strife,
I hit you, I break you, I crush you to nothingness,
And each time you return to life.

Then, behind a frontage of illusion, and with a mask of pretence,
I hide you, but can't reduce you.
Yet in spite of your victory, the false vision of yourself persists.

But when in humility, I bend my head low,
With eyes cast downward, dominating my thoughts,
It is then your turn to be vanquished.

Also Available

By: Akhtarul Wasey,

Farhat Ehsas

376 p.ill.; 22 cm., 2011

ISBN-13: 978-93-5018-081-5

By: Phillip Gowins

vi, 210 p.ill.; 22 cm., 2008

ISBN-13: 978-93-89973-49-0

Sufism and Indian Mysticism

Sufism in Islamic tradition has for centuries been a source of inner peace, spiritual awakening and enlightenment for millions of human beings. It has also been a matter of debate among scholars regarding the questions related to its origin, nature and external manifestations.

This volume, having 29 well researched papers, seeks to present a wide spectrum of perspectives and in-depth studies on different aspects of Islamic Sufism and Indian Mysticism, and their interface, that has manifested itself through the history of Islam's interaction with India, spread over a time-frame of more than a millennium. The contributions in this volume are made by some of the most renowned scholars and experts in the fields of philosophy, Islamic studies, comparative religions, psychology, sociology, history and journalism.

Prof. Akhtarul Wasey is one of the most prominent Islamic scholars and socio-political analysts. He is the Head, Department of Islamic Studies and Director, Zakir Husain Institute of Islamic Studies, Jamia Millia Islamia, New Delhi. He is also editor of three internationally recognized research journals—Islam and Modern Age (English), and Islam Aur Asr-e-Jadeed and Risala Jamia (Urdu). He has served as President of the Dargah Committee, Khwaja Moinuddin Chishti, Ajmer.

Farhat Ehsas (Farhatullah Khan) is one of the leading contemporary Urdu poets, journalists and translators. He has written extensively on socio-cultural and political issues. He is presently Assistant Editor, Islam and Modern Age and Islam Aur Asr-e-Jadeed, the research journals, published by the Zakir Husain Institute of Islamic Studies, Jamia Millia Islamia, New Delhi

Sufism: A Path for Today - The Sovereign Soul

The Aim of the 1,500-Year-Old Spiritual Tradition of Sufism, it has been said, is "the elimination of all veils between man and God." In June 2004, Sufi Master Pir Vilayat Inayat Khan died peacefully at his home in Suresnes, France. As leader of the Sufi Order International which first brought Sufism to the West in 1910, Pir Vilayat had spent more than 40 years teaching this and other truths of Sufism to audiences in the U.S., Europe and Asia.

For 25 years, Sufi teacher Phillip Gowins was able to take advantage of the many visits of Pir Vilayat to the United States. Thus Sufism: A Path for Today-The Sovereign Soul is a homage to the Master, providing as it does an introduction to the ancient stream of wisdom embodied by Sufism—but present in other religions and humanistic philosophies as well— that Pir Vilayat was able to impart to students around the world.

This book is also a description, always concrete, often humorous, of the mystical path that Phillip Gowins himself has pursued over the years. With many examples and exercises, he shows us how we can practise the spiritual life ourselves. The path he lays out is strewn with pitfalls and pleasures alike. He tells us how we can avoid the one and enjoy the other—and attain to love and self-mastery in the increasingly complex 21st century.

PHILLIP GOWINS was born in Minneapolis, Minnesota, in 1945. He has been a cabinetmaker since 1980. In 1979 he met Pir Vilayat Inayat Khan and shortly thereafter was inducted into the Sufi Order in the West. A teacher in that order, he runs a Sufi Center at his home in Yonkers, New York, with his wife, Majida, who is also a teacher. Her daughter, and their grandchildren live with them.

Also Available

Spiritual Liberty

By: Hidayat Inayat-Khan

xvi, 302 p.ill.; 22 cm., 2011
ISBN-13: 978-93-5018-009-9

Based on the teachings of Hazrat Inayat Khan, the founder of International Sufi Movement, this book guides the seeker towards the path and inner realization of true spiritual liberty. And what is spiritual liberty? The book answers:

Spiritual liberty is the path to true religion.

Spiritual liberty is the path to true happiness.

Spiritual liberty is the path to true spirituality.